NO BULLYING

by Alfreda Ragland
illustrated by Bianca Eze

Printed in United States

ISBN: 9798865543008
Independently Published

Hello friends, it's me Lita!
This past week at school,
we learned about bullying.

Bullying is a repetitive pattern of intentional unkind behavior that can cause harm to a person's physical or mental well-being.

Today during circle time, Mrs. Miles posed a question: "Who has been bullied before, and how did it affect you?" Ced was the first to respond. He shared his experience of being bullied by older boys at his previous school.

Ced was bullied daily by classmates who would knock him down, take his lunchbox, and taunt him while others watched and laughed. It became too much for Ced to handle.

quiet out of fear. Mrs. Miles patted him on the back to console him.

Zoey bravely chimed in and revealed that she had also felt the sting of bullying. As the baby of the family, poor Zoey was constantly taunted by her older sister. She teased her about her height and glasses.

Zoey's eyes welled up with tears as she spoke about it. She was deeply hurt because she had always looked up to her older sister. She never expected her own family to cause her such pain. Mrs. Miles comforted Zoey with a pat on the back. "Being unkind to others is never acceptable," Mrs. Miles said to the class.

Ced and Zoey dealt with
bullying differently. Ced kept
it all inside, but Zoey confided
in her parents. This resulted in
her sister facing consequences
for her bad behavior.

"Who has been a bully?" asked Mrs. Miles urging the class to raise our hands. Everyone looked around at each other.

Mrs. Miles put our fears to rest, promising that this time, no one would get into trouble. Instead, she wanted to help us understand how bullying hurts others.

As we glanced around the room, William raised his hand and confessed to having bullied someone.

William pushed his cousin to the ground and hit him multiple times after discovering his favorite toy car was broken. However, he felt remorseful for his actions after hearing Ced and Zoey's feelings about bullying.

He wanted to make it right by telling his cousin he was sorry and deal with whatever punishment his mom would give him.

Mrs. Miles gave William a hug and told him she was proud of him for doing the right thing. She went on to say, "Bullying can cause the other person both mental and physical harm. A person may be so hurt and try to hurt themselves to escape the pain of being bullied."

Mrs. Miles stressed the importance of treating everyone with respect and speaking up if you or someone else experiences mistreatment. No one should be made to feel sad. The class listened seriously.

My heart ached for my friends. I was angry at William at first but I was overjoyed that he realized that what he had done was wrong and wanted to correct his mistakes.

Mrs. Miles had a brilliant idea to lift our spirits –
a group hug. She has always been an empathetic
teacher, and knows just the thing to do when we've
had a challenging day. As lunch time arrived, Mrs.
Miles reminded us of a valuable lesson, "Treat others
the way you want to be treated."
With these words in mind, we left the classroom
feeling even better than when we had arrived.

After lunch, we returned to class and there sat a new student. He introduced himself, but seemed very shy.

At P.E. I noticed he was playing all alone.
I ran up to him and introduced myself.
I asked if I could play basketball with
him, although I was not very good at it.
Lee laughed and said neither am I.
We both laughed and started to play.

A boy named Chris and his friends approached us. "This basketball court is only for big kids and not for little babies!" he yelled. "Go back to the sandbox where you belong," another one screeched. Our feelings were really hurt. I could feel my eyes starting to tear up, but I tried hard not to cry in fear of giving them another reason to joke on us.

I was so upset I just started screaming which made the group of older kids laugh even harder. Ced, William, and Zoey ran over. That didn't stop the older kids. They just turned their attention to my friends. Zoey stood her ground, She started to shout, "Sticks and stones might break our bones, but words will never hurt us," even though she knew better. Mrs. Miles had just taught us about the impact of mean words.

The group of older kids looked really shocked that us smaller kids were standing up to them.

Alarmed by the shouting, Mrs. Miles and Mrs. Davis ran over to us. We told them what happened and what the older kids said. The teachers explained that their behavior was not acceptable and could be considered bullying, a serious issue. We were told to always speak to our teacher when faced with similar situations.

Our principal, Mr. Fox, talked to us and even suggested that the bigger kids teach us how to play basketball.

Mr. Fox Got us together for a celebration and we all made a pact to never bully anyone else. Bullying is the wrong thing to do, even if it seems fun.

Remember, bullying is the wrong thing to do, even if it seems fun. It is important to treat everyone with kindness and respect. Let's all do our part!

ABOUT THE AUTHOR

Alfreda Ragland is the mother of three wonderful children: Jaycen, Jayden, and Kamarie. She also has a fur baby, Prince. Alfreda enjoys reading, shopping, and spending time with family and friends. She has a love for children and is on a mission to encourage and inspire them to love themselves and each other just as God loves us all. She is doing that one book at a time!

ALFREDA RAGLAND

For permission requests, please email:
AuthorAlfredaRagland@gmail.com

Made in United States
Orlando, FL
08 January 2024

42217204R00020